IT'S NOT YOUR FAULT

What To Do When Your Parents Divorce

Rosemary Stones

Illustrated by Belinda Evans

Piccadilly Press • London

For Alan, My Friend

Phototypeset from author's disk by Piccadilly Press.
Printed and bound by Biddles Ltd., Guildford
for the publishers, Piccadilly Press Ltd.,
5 Castle Road, London NW1 8PR

A catalogue record for this book is available from the British
Library.

ISBN: 1 85340 228 1 (hardback)
1 85340 233 8 (trade paperback)

Rosemary Stones lives in South London. She is an editor in a
publishing house. Her books for Piccadilly Press include the
highly-successful *Don't Pick On Me: How to Handle Bullying*.

Belinda Evans graduated from Hull College of Art and Design.
As well as illustrating books, she has a stall in an arts and
crafts market where she sells hand-drawn T-shirts. She
illustrated Rosemary Stones's
Don't Pick On Me.

CONTENTS

Chapter One

WHY DO PARENTS DIVORCE?

"The breakdown of a marriage is obviously a dreadful thing and causes great unhappiness and consternation."
Prince Charles talking in June 1994 about his separation from Princess Diana

"The worst thing about telling the kids was their reactions. My daughter walked out of the room without saying anything. My twelve-year-old cried."
Divorced mother

"I knew it was coming. There'd been a lot of tension and Mum and Dad were always having rows. But that didn't make it easier when they told me. I was scared. I'm used to it now and I'm curious in a way about what's going to happen."
Joel (13)

Every year thousands of parents separate or divorce. If your mum and dad are about to split up or are already separated, you are one of a

1

quarter of all children (over 160,000 in Britain, about a million in the USA) whose families break up while they are still at school.

Knowing that you are one of many children whose parents have separated, rather than thinking that you might be the only one in the world, can be a help. This is because, although no family is quite like any other family and therefore no family breakup will be exactly like another, the feelings and needs of children when their parents are separating or have separated are the same.

You may already have friends or know people at school whose parents have separated; they will understand how painful and difficult this situation is for you.

WHY ARE YOUR PARENTS SEPARATING?

There will be lots of questions you want answers to and things that you have a right to know. But first of all, you probably want to know why your parents are separating. You may think you know why but you need to hear it from them.

Up to this point, your parents may have told you very little about the reasons for their unhappiness and decision to separate. Now you want an explanation. You probably won't like it: unpleasant facts are unpleasant. It's very upsetting to hear your parents say, for example, that they don't enjoy living together any more. But it's better to hear it from them than to spend time worrying about and imagining what might have caused them to split up. You need to be able to make sense of what is going on.

Your parents may say they are separating because:

"we are unhappy living together."

"I can't stand your dad's drinking."
"Mum has met someone else she prefers."
"we've grown apart and we don't have anything in common any more."
"home life is so awful that it can't go on this way."

These are some of the common reasons for parents to separate. You should note that they are all about the relationship between mums and dads. This is important. Parents do not separate because of the things their children do; they separate because things between them as a couple fall apart.

ATTITUDES TO DIVORCE

The sheer number of divorces that take place these days has meant that there has been a great change in society's attitude to divorce. It was once considered very shameful and something that shouldn't be mentioned. Now for the most part, people see divorce as an unfortunate but common occurrence.

The rapid change that has taken place can be seen when you look at the recent history of the British royal family. In the 1950s, the Queen's sister, Princess Margaret, was not allowed to marry the man she loved because he was divorced. In the 1990s, at the time of writing, of the Queen's children, Princess

Anne has divorced and remarried while Princes Charles and Andrew are separated from their wives.

Four-fifths of divorced people remarry and some of these marriages don't last so some children experience not one, but two divorces. A new social pattern called "serial marriage" is beginning to emerge. This means that many adults now marry two or three times in their lifetime.

All this means that the children of divorced parents are so numerous that they will rarely, probably never, be in social situations where they need to worry about social stigma. It also means that it is possible to discuss divorce and its impact on children openly and in a matter-of-fact way. Most importantly, it is now easier to acknowledge that divorce is painful and each family member, both adults and children, will be shocked and full of grief at the end of a marriage.

EVERY FAMILY IS DIFFERENT AND SO IS EVERY DIVORCE

When children are small, they think that every family is just like theirs and that the way their mum and dad organise things is the same in every family. As you get bigger, you begin to realise that friends' families have different ways of doing things and different ways of behaving towards each other.

If your mum and dad always take turns to do the cooking, for example, it can be a shock to discover that in a friend's house, cooking is only done by the mum. If your parents never discuss problems and difficulties, it can be a surprise to find that a friend's mum and dad talk about them together and help each other think about them and sort them out.

Because every family is different, when parents split up, every separation is different too.

Some parents have not been happy together for a long time and their children have grown up in a tense, humourless atmosphere with a mum and dad who hardly speak to each other.

"They were always getting at each other in little ways. Even things like who was going to walk the dog would start them off. I tried to spend as much time out of the house as I could."
Priya (15)

Some mums and dads appear to be getting on fine and the news of their decision to separate comes as a complete surprise and shock to their children.

"I kept thinking this can't be true. If I pretend nothing is wrong and go on doing well at

school, they'll get back together again."
   Jonathan (12)

*"I thought my parents had a wonderful
marriage. They had rows sometimes and
disagreed about things but so did most of my
friends' parents. When I was fifteen I went back
to boarding school for the summer term
thinking everything was wonderful. But one
day I went home for the weekend and my mum
started to cry. She said she and Dad had been
having problems for a long time and she was
going to divorce him. I remember feeling really
angry with her. I thought she wasn't giving my
dad a chance. I also felt that all my happy
childhood up till then had been a lie."*
   Susannah (now 19)

*"When they said they were going to divorce, I
felt as if I'd been kicked in the stomach."*
   Wayne (15)

Some separations are very angry and bitter
with perhaps one parent blaming the other for
everything that has gone wrong.

*"Mum wants me to hate Dad and Dad wants
me to hate Mum. Each of them tells me bad
things about the other. I don't know what to do.
I don't say anything and I feel guilty all the
time."*
   Paul (12)

Other mums and dads manage to separate in a better way, staying friends with each other.

"Dad moved into a flat close by and he comes round a lot for dinner. When Mum goes away, he comes to stay and he looks after us. He and Mum get on fine. She's pleased for him about his new job. Dad even gets on with Trevor, Mum's boyfriend. I was surprised about that."
William (11)

It's good if your parents can still respect each other even if they can't live together any more. Unfortunately, not all mums and dads can manage this.

But however your parents separate, whether it's in a friendly way or in an angry, bitter way, the separation is very upsetting and disturbing for you.

"I knew their marriage wasn't perfect but you could always count on them to be together. I don't feel I can ever trust anyone again."
Helen (14)

"I remember my mother's reaction. I looked into her face and it was covered with tears. I was terrified. I said to myself, 'What's going to happen to me?' The ground went from under me."
Jason (now 16)

WANTING YOUR PARENTS TO STAY TOGETHER

Even if you know that your parents do not treat each other well and are desperately unhappy together, even if they fight and have scenes and scream at each other, part of you probably wants them to stay together. Even if you know that they should separate because things are so unbearable between them and for the family, it's hard to imagine a future when they are no longer together.

If your mum and dad are still friends and still care about each other, it can be even harder to understand why they have decided to separate.

REASONS FOR SEPARATION

So, why do parents separate? Why don't they just try harder to get on and stay together?

Getting married or setting up home together as partners is something that adults do with the highest hopes for happiness ever after. They make a commitment to each other and are serious about wanting the relationship to work. If it then doesn't, they feel great sadness and a sense of failure and loss.

"My parents divorced when I was seven and when I got married I was determined that it was going to work. I wanted to be sure that my children would never have to go through what I went through. When my marriage did break down, I felt I had failed them. I still do."
Gerald (35)

MARRIAGE IS NOT EASY

It is not easy to be married or in a partnership.

This may seem a strange thing to say since so many people in the world are married or plan to get married one day. Almost everyone dreams of having a close, loving relationship with someone special at some point in their adult life.

But getting married or setting up as a partnership, means that two individual people who have had very different upbringings and experiences and who have different needs and hopes, think that they can find a way to stay together happily – for ever. And these days, when people live longer on average, married life can last fifty years or more...

To be married successfully or to be in a successful partnership, these adults need to know how to be half of a couple while at the same time remaining separate, individual people. It's like being part of a team but at the same time being an individual player.

This is a difficult juggling act and lots of adults don't manage it, or don't manage it well.

HAPPY MARRIAGES?

It's always hard to know quite what someone's marriage is like because a lot of the important bits go on in private.

But if you know a family where you think the mum and dad are happy together, you'll probably have noticed that they like each other's company, they are affectionate towards each other, they seem to appreciate and understand each other. They probably don't do these things all the time – even the best marriages have ups and downs – but they do them enough for their children to feel safe and secure. In a family like this, there is usually a lot of laughter and fun.

Some adults have an unhappy marriage but they don't know how to make it better. They are afraid to separate so they just put up with it. The result can be utter misery for everyone with a home atmosphere that is tense, loveless, humourless and barren. If your home life is like this, you know how draining, troubling and sad it can be.

Some parents have a violent relationship which can be downright dangerous for their children. Family breakup in this case gives hope for a new and better life.

MAKING A MARRIAGE WORK

One of the most important things in making a

marriage or a partnership work is for the people in them to be able to face differences and problems in a good way.

Two adults who live together as a couple and then start a family by having a child, have to be able to work out disagreements and share responsibility equally.

It sounds so simple, but unfortunately it's very hard to do. Sometimes parents can't do it because their own parents (your grandparents) didn't have good ways of dealing with problems and weren't able to help your parents learn how to do it. People of your grandparents' age were often taught that you had to stay married even if you weren't happy. In that situation, problems and differences were often just ignored or endured and everyone hoped that they would go away. This was not a good model for your parents.

Sometimes parents get together very young and they haven't had enough adult experience to help them sort things out well.

Sometimes parents get on very well for a number of years and, like everyone else, they continue to develop their interests and grow as people. But if they happen to develop and grow in different ways they may find they are no longer compatible.

Sometimes parents discover that they don't, after all, have enough in common and no amount of trying to fix it will improve things.

What happens when parents are unhappy? The next chapter discusses what effect this can have on family life and on children.

Chapter Two

LIFE WITH UNHAPPY PARENTS

SEPARATION HURTS

Whether your mum and dad are married or whether they are living together as partners, when they decide to separate it means that everything you have always taken for granted about home life comes to an end. This is very distressing and frightening however old you are when it happens.

Whether you are four or nine or thirteen or eighteen, seeing your mum and dad split up is something that touches you very deeply. This is quite normal. Even people in their twenties and beyond can be deeply affected when their parents split up – and they are grown-ups.

"I can see it now. Dad was wearing jeans and a blue sweatshirt. Mum was nervous and she sat on the edge of the chair. Dad stammered a lot and finally said, 'Mum and I don't love each other any more. I'll be moving out next week to live in a flat in town.' I jumped up and ran out

screaming, 'hate you!' "
  Sara (now 17)

"I knew Dad was planning to leave Mum and live with Anne. But then he bought Mum a necklace. It cost a lot, £39.99. When he did that I was so excited; I thought it meant he was going to stay. But he didn't."
  Michelle (9)

The breakup of a family is a kind of bereavement and feelings of anger, fear, guilt and disappointment are to be expected.

"I was nine when they divorced. I used to crawl into bed and hide under the duvet to shut out what was happening."
  Patrick (now 15)

MARRIAGE GUIDANCE

Of course some parents who are unhappy together try to find out what the problems are and what they can do about them by seeking professional help from a marriage guidance counsellor. The counsellor may, or may not, be able to help them to stay together in a better way. Sometimes it becomes clear that a marriage cannot be saved and the counsellor's job is then to help the parents to separate in as friendly and caring a way as possible.

KEEPING THE SHOW ON THE ROAD

When parents who live together don't know
how to sort out disagreements and difficulties
and are unable or unwilling to seek
professional help for their problems, they have
to find some way of coping which keeps family
life going. Often, though, it isn't a very good
way and it isn't going to solve anything.

If you are a child with unhappy parents, you probably won't know or be told quite what the problem is between them. But even if they try to hide their difficulties from you, you will probably pick up that something is wrong. Everyone is sensitive to an atmosphere that is tense, troubled, fearful, cold or awkward.

Here are some of the strategies that parents use to try to cope with their problems when they are not able to sort them out together in a good way. Perhaps you will recognize some of these:

1. FIGHTS AND ROWS

Rows occur in all families between parents and they can be a good thing if they are occasional and one-off. Good rows are ways to let off steam and clear the air. Everyone feels better afterwards.

But some parents do not have good rows. These parents argue and fight and abuse each other constantly. Sometimes they shout insults at each other but sometimes the abuse is physical. Perhaps dad hits mum or pushes her about.

Children who grow up in emotionally or physically violent families with parents like these are constantly frightened; they often try to protect one parent from another or try to keep the peace. This is a terrible strain and not a child's job. If your parents behave like this,

you will probably feel more relieved than sad
when they separate. You will also be full of
hope that the future will be better.

2. AVOIDANCE

Sometimes unhappy parents avoid differences
and problems by avoiding each other even
though they live together in the same house.
They do this by not speaking to each other or
by not listening to each other. Mum may not
speak to dad for a week; dad may disappear to
the pub every evening rather than listen to
mum.

Parents like these allow their angry and resentful feelings towards each other to build up – even if mum is not speaking to dad she is thinking angrily all week about whatever he has done to upset her. While they are busy not talking and not listening to each other, these parents are allowing a gulf to grow between them so that even talking things through becomes impossible.

If your parents behave like this, you should try not to let them use you to carry messages between them. "Tell him/her yourself!" is a good thing to say if you can manage it.

3. GIVING WAY

For a marriage or partnership to work, each parent has to be prepared to adapt to the other to some extent or life together will be impossible. If dad wants a purple bathroom suite and mum wants a green one, one parent will have to adapt to the other unless they can afford two bathrooms. Alternatively, they might agree to choose white which they both like. If both parents are prepared to adapt and compromise, differences between them can be worked out.

But in some marriages or partnerships, it's always the same person who gives way. If dad always adapts to whatever mum wants, then mum makes all the decisions about what happens in the family. Dad's feelings are never taken into account and mum has to take on all the responsibility. This is not a good or fair way for two grown-ups to behave towards each other and resentment will grow.

4. TRIANGLES

Parents sometimes get involved with someone or something else when they are not getting on well together. Your dad may become obsessed with work, staying late at the office every night and bringing work home at weekends. Your mum may start a relationship with another man. This is known as a "triangle" and it is a way for unhappy parents to get away from some of the tensions and pressures of their marriage.

Sometimes, and this can be very confusing for you, the triangle may consist of your parents and you. As your parents aren't getting on well with each other they may start to focus all their attention on you, worrying constantly about you and not allowing you to take any steps towards independence.

UNHELPFUL WAYS OF COPING

All parents, whether they are about to split up or not, do some of the things described above some of the time – giving way too much, rowing, sulking, focusing on other things and people. It's when parents really aren't getting on that tension increases and these unhelpful ways of coping with difficulties can become chronic and quite unbearable.

WHAT HAPPENS IN YOUR FAMILY?

Ask yourself these questions about how your parents deal with difficulties and problems. Ask them first about one parent, then the other.

When there is a problem does she/does he :
1) change the subject?
2) leave the room?
3) go silent?
4) develop a headache or other illness?
5) shout and scream?
6) cry?
7) think of someone to blame?
8) ask you (or your brother/sister) to sort it out?
9) get depressed?
10) take alcohol or drugs?
11) reach for a cream cake?
12) discuss calmly what the best course of action is?

Your answers may help you to see your parents' way of coping, and how it works, more clearly.

SHOULD YOUR MUM AND DAD STAY TOGETHER FOR YOUR SAKE?

As I've said before, however awful home life is with parents who row or don't talk to each other, you probably find the idea of your mum and dad splitting up very disturbing and frightening. Should your parents stay together for your sake?

Parents who want to separate are inevitably very preoccupied with their own feelings of pain and unhappiness. Even so, most parents spend a lot of time worrying about how a separation will affect their children and what to do for the best in this difficult situation.

Is it better for a child to live with one of them in a peaceful atmosphere or is it better for the child if they stay together even though s/he will be brought up in an unhappy, warring atmosphere?

CHILDREN HAVE NO CONTROL

The difficulty for you in this situation is that, although you can tell your parents again and again that you want them to stay together, you have no control over their decision. You cannot make your parents stay together if one or both of them decide that this is not what they want.

When children are small, they think their parents have no other function than to be their mum and dad. As you grow bigger, you begin to

23

understand that your parents do and are lots of things that don't relate directly to you, even though they care passionately about you. Your dad might be crazy about golf or animal liberation; your mum might love rock-climbing or have a big circle of friends she likes to see. You begin, gradually, to see your parents not just as parents, but as people who are your parents.

Because your parents are people, they each
have their life to lead and only they can choose
how to do this. If one, or both, of your parents
is unhappy in their marriage or partnership
and believes that a separation is for the best,
you have no choice but to accept this.

YES, THEY ARE GOING TO SEPARATE

Your parents tell you they are going to
separate. That's very, very hard. Of course you
will feel great distress – this is quite normal.

The next chapter will discuss your feelings,
what worries you may have and what you can
do about them.

Chapter Three

WHAT HAPPENS WHEN PARENTS SEPARATE?

When parents separate it is rarely a complete surprise to their children. More often, the relationship between the parents has been going wrong for some time, perhaps several years, and you are already well aware that things "feel" different at home.

"Mum will be chatting away happily until Dad walks through the door. Then she will hardly say a word and she goes all stiff."
Mairead (10)

"When I was little Mum and Dad used to have fun and do a lot of teasing. Now they hardly even look at each other."
Billy (8)

"It seems like nothing Dad does is right any more. Mum can't find a good word to say to him."
Kate (12)

You probably already know children whose parents are separated or divorced and you may have been fearful for a long time that this might happen to your parents. Perhaps you have asked your parents if they are planning to split up or tried to pick up clues by listening to conversations.

"I didn't know what was going on. I didn't want to ask awful questions and hear awful answers."
Lizzie (9)

All this uncertainty is very alarming and upsetting. It would be more reassuring for children if parents who are still making up their minds whether to separate or how to separate were able to say something like:
"We aren't happy together any more. We are discussing what to do about it. When we decide, we will let you know straight away. In the meantime, please try not to worry about it."

In practice, many parents find it hard to admit to their children that they want to separate and that their marriage or partnership has failed. They may feel guilty and full of distress that they have failed you. They may feel unable to talk about what is happening without being bitter, hostile, judgmental and accusing towards each other.

27

They may not know how to start talking to you about it.

In this situation there are some ways you can help yourself to cope with these frustrations:

1) Talk to someone you trust. Do you have a friend at school whose parents are divorced? Is there a school counsellor you like? Do you have brothers or sisters of the right age that you can talk to?

2) Write yourself a list of "What Ifs": What if my parents separate? What if they stay together without getting on any better? What if I live with just my mum? What if I can't see my dad? Get all your questions down on paper so that if there is a good moment to ask them you are already prepared.

3) Let your parents know that you would like to discuss what is going on, that not knowing is causing you great anxiety.

ANNOUNCING THE SEPARATION

Once your parents have decided to separate, you should be told as soon as possible.

For some parents this decision is the end of a long period of mutual upheaval, argument and soul-searching. For other parents, it may have come as a terrible shock; sometimes one partner simply announces out of the blue that s/he is leaving.

But whatever circumstances lead to your parents' separation, for you this event is the beginning of a new kind of life. Parts of it will probably remain the same but other aspects will change altogether.

Most parents, when they separate, do their best to explain to their children what is going to happen practically and to talk about the sadness and pain that everyone feels.

In an ideal world it would be good if your parents could tell you together what their plans are for the separation and for the future.

Unfortunately, some parents feel so angry with each other that they are not able to stay in the same room together long enough to do this without shouting at each other. If your parents are like this, it would be good if you could ask them separately to explain things so that you can hear both sides of the story.

Some children are unlucky. Their parents are either so preoccupied with their own feelings of distress or are too selfish to think enough about the feelings and needs of their children during and after family breakup. Some parents just don't know how to treat their children in this situation so they do nothing. It's hard for these children to feel secure and cared about. If this is happening to you, you may be able to find a sympathetic adult to talk to – your teacher perhaps, or your grandparents.

When some parents are breaking up, the situation becomes so stressful that one parent simply leaves. If this has happened to you, it can be particularly upsetting. It's easy to assume that your mum/dad can't love and care about you if s/he takes off in this way.

It may be that your mum/dad isn't very good at caring but it could also be that they are under so much stress that they just aren't able to do any better at the moment. Hopefully, they will find a way to get in touch when things are calmer.

When you are first told that your parents are going to separate it will be a shock even if you suspected it might happen. At the same time, you may have a feeling of relief that something you have dreaded happening for so long, has now actually happened.

IS ONE PARENT TO BLAME?

It may be that your parents are separating because one of them behaves in a violent, frightening or utterly impossible way that you have witnessed many times. Perhaps your dad hits your mum or your mum has a drink problem that she refuses to get help with. If this is the case for you, the shock of your parents' separation may not be as great because you will have seen it coming. You will probably feel great relief not to be in that situation any more and full of hope that your life can now be happier.

But there are also parents who upset their partner deeply in other ways – perhaps your dad has lots of girlfriends and this hurts your mum or your mum seems to care more about political causes than spending time with your dad and he feels unwanted. Problems like these are, however, your parent's problems, not yours.

DON'T TAKE SIDES

Whatever your parents think about each other is their business and it is quite wrong for one of them to try to make you their ally against the other parent.

Perhaps your mum does spend too much time on political issues (you probably wish she didn't), but you still love her. Perhaps your dad is a womaniser (you wish he wasn't), but you still love him. You can love both your parents even if they don't love each other any more.

It is also possible that you only know half the story when your parents break up. You might be terribly angry with you dad for leaving your mum for another woman without being aware that he has spent years trying to improve and save the marriage. You might be angry with you mum for neglecting your dad in favour of other interests without being aware that all her efforts to include or involve him in things were endlessly rebuffed.

In this fraught situation it is not useful for you to try to blame one parent or the other for what has happened. Marriage breakdown is not usually something that one parent does to another but is the result of what happens between them as a couple.

You may understand perfectly well that your parents' marriage was disastrous and could not have continued, but a terrible husband or terrible wife is not necessarily a terrible dad or terrible mum. You have every right to keep seeing both your mum and your dad even if they don't want to see each other. Your parents must not try to make you take sides in what is their quarrel.

PRACTICALLY, WHAT ARE YOUR PARENTS' PLANS?

You need to know exactly what is happening and when it is happening if that has been decided. Here are some of the kinds of things you will want to ask:

1) Is Mum or Dad moving out?
2) Which parent will I be living with?
3) What are the arrangements for me to see the parent I am not living with?
4) Will I have to move house?
5) Will I have to move school?
6) Who will drive me to swimming?
7) What will happen to the cat?
8) Who will help with my Maths?
9) Do my grandparents know?
10) Are you going to get a divorce?
11) Has my teacher been told?
12) What shall I tell my friends?

13) Will my brothers/sisters and I all stay together?

GRANDPARENTS AND MORE

When parents separate or divorce, children can sometimes find they lose a whole side of their family.

For example, if your dad moves out and you are only able to visit him occasionally, the ties that bind you to his parents (your grandparents) and to his sisters and brothers (your aunts and uncles) can weaken. Gradually you can find yourself deprived of a large chunk of your "extended" family with all that that means in terms of shared history, people and connections.

If you are in a stepfamily and your parent and their partner separate you may also be in danger of losing people who are a very important part of your life.

This can cause great sadness:

"From the day my parents divorced, I felt I had lost not just my father but a whole family. I go and see Dad but I hardly see the rest of his family."
Jan (11)

"My grandparents saw us a few times after Mum and Dad split up but they had to arrange

it with Mum and they'd never got on well. After a bit, I suppose they gave up."

Colin (13)

"Mum has a brother who is great. He always used to bring us little presents and mess about. Now we don't see him any more."

Tom (9)

"Mum remarried when I was twelve but when I was fifteen that marriage broke up too. I wasn't too upset that my stepfather was leaving as I'd never felt close to him but I wanted him to leave his children with us. They were my brother and sister. The day they packed their clothes we were all crying. I also miss my step-grandmother. She was good fun."

Katy (now 17)

If you are in this situation, you can make it clear to your parents that your grandparents, your stepfamily and the rest of your "extended family" are important to you and you want to keep in touch with them and for them to keep in touch with you. You could also make the effort to keep in touch with them without always going through your parents.

No doubt your grandparents very much want to keep in touch with you. However, if you are living with your mother, for instance, and your father is their son, they may feel it's disloyal to your dad to make contact with your mother in order to arrange to see you. Your stepfamily may also worry about how best to keep in touch with you.

Problems like this need to be talked about and sensible solutions found if important relationships are not to be lost or neglected.

There may not be a problem. Some grand-parents are very good at not taking sides when mums and dads separate and good at keeping in touch with their grandchildren. They know how to provide a strong family network that can go on working and keep the different generations in touch even after a divorce. Some parents and stepparents are also good at contriving ways for children to keep in touch with the people who care about them and to whom they are important.

SO, HOW DOES IT FEEL?

When your parents split up your world is disrupted in a major way. Your parents don't want or mean to do this but it's an inevitable by-product of their separation. Even if they are the kind of parents who can work together to organise things as well and sensibly as circumstances allow, you will be wondering: "Now that this has happened, can I ever trust my parents again?"

The next chapter discusses worries such as this and takes a look at how you will be feeling now that you know that your parents are separating.

Chapter Four

HOW IT FEELS WHEN PARENTS SEPARATE

HOW IT FEELS STRAIGHT AFTER THE SEPARATION

When you are first told about the separation you may find yourself saying all kinds of angry, hurtful things to your parents:

"I hate you."
"It's all your fault."

Or you may feel so frightened that you beg them to stay together:

"If I'm good, will you change your mind?"

Or you may feel so shocked that you can't take in what is being said and you can't bear to hear any more:

"I don't want to know about it."

All these reactions are quite normal. You need to be able to pour out your feelings. Hopefully, your parents will understand this and be able to listen to you. It's good if they can – they need to know how hurt you feel so that they can care for you and help you get over the initial shock.

When your feelings are in such a state of turmoil, it's important that you admit this to yourself instead of pretending that it's all cool and you can handle it.

Here are some of the feelings that may be giving you trouble:

1. DISBELIEF

Arguments and rows between your parents may have happened so frequently that you thought of them as a part of normal family life. Perhaps your parents often used to threaten to leave each other though they never actually did. You eventually stopped paying attention when they had rows because you were so used to it.

Now that your parents really have separated, you just can't believe it. It feels like a bad dream. Perhaps tomorrow everything will be back to normal.

If this has happened to you, it will take a while for the knowledge to sink in that what has happened is permanent: your parents have left each other and they are almost certainly not going to get back together again.

This state of disbelief and shock will have to be worked through before you will be able to take stock of your situation and plan for your new life. You may find it helpful to talk through your feelings with a sympathetic friend or teacher, or perhaps a counsellor.

2. GUILT

When parents separate, small children of three to five years old often think that they are responsible for splitting up their parents. They imagine that if they had made less noise or tidied up their toys before going to bed, mum or dad would not have left.

In the normal course of growing up, all children feel hostile at times to one or other of their parents and want to have the other parent all to themselves. A little girl, for example, might wish that her mother would disappear so that she can have her father all to herself. If the mother then leaves because the marriage has broken down, it can appear to the small child that her wish has come true and she is guilty of breaking up the marriage.

Children of your age know rationally and logically that your parents' splitting up has everything to do with their inability to get on with each other and nothing at all to do with your behaviour. But, however sensibly you try to think about it, some part of you may be agonising that perhaps in some way it is your fault.

Perhaps you've been moody at home, irritating everyone by playing Heavy Metal

music at high volume; perhaps you've been messing about at school and you've heard your parents quarrelling about your bad school report. Are you the straw that broke the camel's back? Would it have been different if you had followed all the rules your parents set down?

Even if your behaviour has been mega-irritating for everyone, it is not powerful enough to destroy the relationship between your parents. Even if, say, your father's departure from the family home occurred following a row with your mother about you and your behaviour, it's important to remember that he would not have stormed out if his relationship with your mother were not already in a fragile state. It is irrelevant that you happened to be the subject of the quarrel.

Sometimes some parents, in their unhappiness, cast about thoughtlessly for someone to blame when their marriage fails:

"Maybe if you'd behaved better than you're doing now, your mum/dad wouldn't have left."

If a parent lashes out in this way, it's hard not to take to heart what has been said in the heat of the moment. Remember though, that adults are grown-up people who choose how to behave. If their marriages break up they have no one to blame (if blame has to be found) but themselves.

Usually children feel guilty and responsible for their parents' difficulties because they don't know what is undermining the marriage. If you don't know what is happening between your parents, it's tempting to think that it may be something to do with you, because that at least provides some kind of logical explanation. But remember, even if you're the subject of your parents' arguments, you are not the cause. Why not ask them straight out why they are separating and set your mind at rest?

3. LACK OF TRUST AND FEELINGS OF ANGER

You may well be wondering if you can ever trust your parents (or anyone else), again.

Foremost in your mind may be the thought that if your parents, who once loved each other enough to get together and start a family, can separate, perhaps they're capable of binning you too. If your parents don't love each other any more, or don't love each other enough to stay together, how do you know they still love you?

You may also be full of rage with your parents:

"Why couldn't they get their act together instead of messing up my life?"
"How dare Dad leave Mum and go and live with Paula."
"How dare Mum chuck Dad out. If she can do that to him, will she do that to me if I annoy her?"

Perhaps, in the heat of the moment, you've told your parents that you hate them. How can they possibly love you after that?

What you have to remember is that the ties between parent and child, child and parent endure forever. Husbands and wives can stop being married, partners can split up, but you will always be your parents' child and they will always be your parents. A bond as strong as this should be and is capable of weathering many storms.

These are some of the feelings that children often experience immediately after their parents separate. This can be a highly frustrating and confusing time because you are in the position of being at the receiving end of other people's decisions over which you have no control. You cannot stop your mum and dad separating; you cannot prevent them doing whatever they plan to do.

All you can do in this situation is be patient and see what happens. You won't know whether your parents' new arrangements are going to make you feel comfortable and secure until you've tested them out and this is going to take a matter of months rather than weeks.

The newness and shock of the separation will wear off eventually and be replaced with acceptance and healing. Don't worry too much about feeling angry, upset, guilty, unsure and depressed about the future. It's normal. (But if these feelings threaten to overwhelm you, seek help. There is a list of organisations that offer help at the end of the book.)

You need to work through your immediate feelings of grief and loss before you can begin to feel like your old self again.

ONGOING PROBLEMS

Sometimes children whose parents have separated worry about what other people will think; they feel ashamed and insecure about their situation. Here are some of the problems that you may face in the longer term:

1. EMBARRASSMENT

"I was eleven when my parents divorced and I felt ashamed and humiliated. It was my mother who left with a boyfriend nine years younger than she was. I couldn't believe it. My mother!"
Louise (now 16)

Sometimes a child whose parents have separated imagines that they have "child from a broken home" written all over them. They feel ashamed about their situation and feel they have to hide it.

Rationally you might know that separation and divorce are extremely common (in the UK one in three marriages ends in the divorce courts), but perhaps you don't happen to know anyone in that situation and you suddenly feel very exposed, as though everyone is looking at you.

If you have this feeling of strain about your social relationships outside the home – in your neighbourhood, with friends, at school, etc. – it can be very exhausting. Try to remember that people know you and think about you as a person in your own right, not just as your parents' child or as part of a family. You are just as welcome in all these places as you were before. Your new "status" as a child from a "broken" home does not in any way impact on your identity.

It is also possible that people are more used to dealing with and accepting "shocking" events and changes (divorce, money problems, redundancy, failing exams, suicide, illness and so forth) than you imagine and that they will be understanding and kind rather than judgmental.

2. ANGER AND LOSS

You may be feeling angry and disorientated because the loss of family life as you have known it till now has not come about through some tragic accident or fatal illness but because your parents (or at least one of them) deliberately and voluntarily decided to separate.

When your parents split up it can almost feel as though there has been a death in the family, particularly if one parent leaves to live far away. And yet, all the sympathy and care you could expect if a parent had died and all the understanding about feelings of loss, do not come your way. Instead you're expected to get on with life at school and elsewhere as though nothing had happened. No wonder you feel angry.

If you haven't got a sympathetic person to talk to about these troubling feelings, it may help to keep a diary in which you write down how you feel.

3. LOSS OF POWER

Some children feel that the fact that one of their parents has left, reflects badly on them, as though it were able to weaken or damage them in some way. If his father has left, a boy may feel this makes him less masculine. If a mother leaves, a girl may feel confused and inadequate about her femininity.

What you need to remember is that, although a father represents maleness and a mother represents femaleness to their children, you can choose to be male or female in your own way. Look around at other adults you respect and see how they conduct themselves as men or as women. There are sure to be good ways of doing things that you can relate to.

4. TEASING

It's a good idea to tell people that your parents are separating. Of course an unpleasant or malicious "friend" can be quick to realise that your parents' separation is upsetting you and use it as a weapon to tease you. If this happens, remember that this teasing is no different from being teased for being short or for wearing braces on your teeth and the strategies to deal with it should be the same, that is:

1) Try not to show that you are upset. If teasers don't get a reaction, they stop teasing.

2) Imagine that your head is enclosed in a giant bubble. Each nasty tease just bounces off the bubble without getting through to you.

3) Remember that bullies and teasers often tease or bully about things that frighten them. Teasing or bullying is their way of coping with them.

5. FEAR OF LOSING TOUCH WITH AN ABSENT PARENT

If your mum or dad has left to set up a new home with someone else or if s/he has moved far away, you may be afraid that you will lose touch with her/him. It's hard to maintain a good, relaxed relationship with a parent whom you don't see every day.

Many parents who no longer live with their children also worry desperately about how to keep in touch in a good way and say how sad they feel not to see their child growing up from day to day.

Sadly, many separated fathers do lose contact with their children within two years of the separation. If this has happened to you, it is a great sadness. It may be that when you are older, you will be able to find a way to make contact with your father again.

How easy, or difficult, it is to maintain contact with your absent parent will usually depend on whether your parents separated in a bitter or an amicable way. Hopefully, however they feel about each other, they will understand that you need to have regular contact with both of them.

Keeping in touch also involves effort and thought – ringing up regularly, writing, sending postcards, creating opportunities to meet up, planning holidays well in advance. You can play an active role in all of this.

6. CONFUSION OVER SCHOOL MATTERS

As far as school is concerned, it would be sensible for your parents to inform your form teacher or housemaster or whichever teacher has overall care for you, that they have separated. If they haven't, ask them to tell the school. These days, teachers know a good deal about the impact of divorce on children and they will be understanding and supportive to you, particularly if you find it hard to concentrate and are not able to give of your best for a while.

"After school I go to my room and play loud music. I think it stops me feeling anything."
  Martin (14)

"I feel like I'm going through the motions. I go to school. I don't pay much attention to what is going on. It doesn't seem very important any more. My marks have got bad."
  Rebecca (13)

It's quite common for children in your situation who have had to use so much emotional energy to cope with their parents' separation, to find that their school work suffers for a while, however hard they try. If this happens to you, it is a stage that will pass as you gradually get used to the changes in your life. You will get back on form.

  Your parents also need to agree, if they are able to do so, on a system to keep each other informed about your school activities, special events, reports, etc. It would be sensible of them to let the school know which parent to send reports to or to let them know that both parents should be sent them independently.

  It will also make life easier for you if your parents can agree either to take it in turns to attend school events, exeats, etc. or to attend together in a relaxed and peaceful way. The last thing you want at sports day is your mum and dad squabbling over you in public.

It may not have occurred to your parents to think through these school issues yet. They matter to you, though, so why not draw their attention to them?

7. FEAR ABOUT YOUR OWN RELATIONSHIPS

Now that you have seen your parents split up, you may be afraid that you are in some way contaminated by failure and that when you are grown up, you won't be able to have a good, lasting relationship with someone special.

It's true that divorce has a profound effect on children but it does not follow that if you are the child of divorced parents, you will not be able to make good relationships in the future.

Whether or not divorce occurs in your family, it is the kind of family you come from and the way its members relate to each other that will influence who you become.

If divorce occurs in your family, the way that that divorce is conducted is significant in terms of how negative its impact is on you. Recent research suggests that more problems result for children if they have to witness high levels of conflict, hostility, anger and tension during the events. However, high levels of conflict can also be present in families where parents have no intention of separating.

If you are the child of divorced parents, there is the temptation to interpret divorce as resulting in an "unsuccessful" family, a "failure". But how can it have been unsuccessful or a "failure" if it resulted in you? Something good came out of it.

It is also possible that something positive

will come out of divorce for your parents. This is not always so and not necessarily the case for both of them, but it is possible that they will have learnt a lot about themselves from the breakup of their relationship and be in a stronger position to go on and find something good for themselves in the future.

It is easier to make good relationships in adult life if you have had the opportunity as a child to observe a good relationship in action and learn how it is done – in particular how conflicts and problems can be solved in a positive way. Perhaps you know some adults who seem to have a happy and nurturing marriage or partnership – uncles, aunts, the parents of friends. It is also good to observe how some adults (perhaps your parents) are able to learn from their mistakes and move on in a positive and sustaining way.

Unfortunately some parents are not able to do this. They go on repeating the same mistakes or they allow what has happened to poison their life. If your mum or dad is like this, it's hard to watch. There is nothing, though, that you can do about it. Your parents are grown-up people who choose how to behave and it is not, in any case, a child's job to try and sort out her/his parents.

It's important not to get confused about this in the aftermath of a separation or divorce. It is a parent's job to look after their children, help them sort out problems and learn gradually to become independent. But if a separation is very traumatic, a parent might begin to rely on the child for support and care.

It can be heartbreaking to see a parent whom you love in a state of anguish and distress and of course you want to help but this "role reversal" (the child looking after the parent) should not be allowed to continue indefinitely. If your parent cannot get back on their feet, s/he should seek professional help, not rely on you.

The next chapter explains how arrangements are made for where and with whom you will live and how you can influence those decisions.

Chapter Five

SEPARATION, DIVORCE AND AFTER

THE LAW IN ENGLAND AND WALES

People who are married to each other can only get divorced if their marriage has irretrievably broken down. "Irretrievable" means "cannot be repaired" and the irretrievable breakdown of a marriage therefore means that nothing can be done to repair the marriage and make it work.

For the divorce to be granted by the court, the person who wants the divorce has to prove one or more of five facts about the marriage. These "facts" include whether one or both partners has committed adultery (had a sexual relationship with someone else) or behaved unreasonably (for example, been violent; gambled away all the money); whether one partner deserted another for a period of two years; whether the couple have been separated for two years by consent; whether the couple have been separated for five years even though one partner does not want a divorce.

Of course some parents separate and don't

get round to divorcing for some time. If they want a "no fault" divorce, your parents will in any case have to have lived apart for two years. If they are going for a divorce on other grounds, it can happen more quickly.

Even if you have got used to your parents living apart, you will probably find it quite upsetting if and when they decide to divorce. Some part of you may have been clinging on to the idea that they might get back together again and the divorce puts an end to these hopes. It is also very probable that your parents, however much they want to divorce, will also feel sad about it. A divorce brings to an end a relationship that was once full of hope and the expectation of happiness.

CHILDREN AND DIVORCE

Parents who separate without divorcing can make their own decisions about arrangements for your care and support following the separation without reference to the courts unless one of them applies to the court for wardship.

If your parents were married to each other when or after you were born, both automatically have *parental* responsibility for you when they divorce. This means that both parents have the responsibility and right to create the best solution for your care following family breakdown.

When your parents separate, one of the most important and difficult decisions that has to be made is which parent you will live with. In practice the parent who currently has day-to-day care for you (the parent you live with) will be in a stronger position to make choices about your upbringing. This parent will be responsible for seeing that you have everything you need (shelter, education, food, love, support, etc.) following the separation or divorce. The other parent will be expected to contribute financially to your upkeep while you are in full-time education and to take an active interest in your welfare.

If your parents are able to agree between themselves about which parent you should live with and when the other parent should see you, then it is likely that no formal court order will be made. Obviously this means that parents have to be able to cooperate sensibly with each other in your best interests.

If, in the future, your parents cannot agree about something to do with you, under the Children Act of 1989, one or both of them can apply for a section 8 order to be applied. The district judge can then ask for a welfare report to be prepared or for your parents to attend a court hearing.

When parents cannot agree about what arrangements are best, under section 8 of the Children Act the court will make a *residence order*. This order settles the arrangements about who a child will live with. Usually it is with one parent but a residence order can allow for shared parenting. This means that children divide their time equally between their parents' homes.

Sunday - Wednesday am

Wednesday pm - Saturday

The court will also grant a *contact order*. This requires the parent you are living with to allow the other parent to keep in touch with you. Contact can take the form of visits or stop-overs or letters or phone calls or all or some of these.

TAKING YOUR VIEWS INTO ACCOUNT

However residence and contact are decided, they are supposed to be in your best interests – that is to ensure that you are happy and secure and properly cared for. Obviously, your opinion on what arrangements should be made matters a great deal and your parents should consult you. If a court welfare officer becomes involved, s/he will also want to know what you think, as will the judge. Your wishes won't necessarily be granted but they are more likely to be if you let everyone know what they are.

SPEAKING UP FOR YOURSELF

If you get on with both your parents (and even if you don't), it is very hard to say what your preferences are without feeling disloyal to one or the other. Sometimes children feel that they have to "look after" one of their parents and they elect to live with her/him rather than with the parent they really want to live with.

"I felt like a traitor when I said I wanted to live with Mum. But I don't like Dad's girlfriend."
   Anna (12)

"I said I wanted to live with both my parents."
   Eddie (10)

At this point you need to look after yourself. Think about where you feel most secure and comfortable. If you feel strongly about which parent you want to live with, go for that. Often the decision will be made for you and in some ways this may be easier to cope with.

If there is a court hearing, the judge may ask to see you on your own in private to talk to you and ask what you would like to happen.

The older you are, the more likely the court welfare officer and judge are to take your views on board. The views of children from around ten years and upwards who have good reasons for their preferences, will often be decisive. On the other hand, if the judge or welfare officer suspects that your mum or your dad has been putting pressure on you, your "opinion" will not carry much weight.

SPLITTING UP CHILDREN
The splitting up of a family is almost always considered a bad thing and wherever possible arrangements are made so that sisters and

brothers, sometimes even half-sisters and half-brothers, can stay together.

RISK OF HARM
It may be very clear which parent should have residence. If one parent has behaved in a violent or abusive way or has, for example, a serious alcohol problem, residence will undoubtedly be awarded to the other parent.

GAY PARENTS

In the past, the courts have been prejudiced against gay parents even in cases where there was evidence of good parenting and a strong bond between parent and child. Today, homosexuality is still considered negatively but it is no longer a decisive factor. If you have a gay parent, s/he would be wise to obtain professional advice from a solicitor experienced in this area.

PARENTAL CAPABILITY

Sometimes a parent is just not well placed to have residence – your mum may have to travel a lot for work; your dad may work on an oil rig. If you have brothers or sisters of preschool age, it may mean that the parent who has residence is the one who can more easily stay at home.

A parent who can offer a stable home life will usually have a stronger claim to have residence than an unreliable parent. If, for example, your dad suddenly left your mum and disappeared for three months with a girlfriend, he would not be in a strong position to have residence since he has clearly not made the interests of his children a priority.

If relatives, perhaps your gran or an aunt, or other people (e.g. a childminder, a nanny) are involved in bringing you up, the court will take this into account in deciding on the best arrangements. These days the courts are very much more flexible in accepting the diversity of family arrangements that can work well. If, for example, your mum and dad have always gone out to work and your gran has looked after you, the court is likely to take the view that you should continue to be cared for by your grandmother.

THE LAW IN SCOTLAND

The Children Act of 1989 does not apply in Scotland, but many aspects of the proceedings in England and Wales, described above, are very similar to proceedings in Scotland.

Parents in Scotland are considered to be *joint guardians* and to have *joint custody* of their children. When parents divorce, it is unusual for guardianship to be altered. A parent wanting *sole custody* has to apply to the court for this. It is usually awarded to the parent who is to have day-to-day care for the children.

Arrangements for care and access are usually worked out between the parents. The court will intervene if the arrangements break down and, possibly, regulate *access* by the parent with whom the children do not live.

THE LAW IN NORTHERN IRELAND
The Children Act of 1989 does not apply in Northern Ireland where the principles of custody and access are used.

QUESTIONS YOU SHOULD ASK
Because there can be such a lot of uncertainty around divorce and the arrangements about which parent you will live with and how and when you will see the other parent, you will need to be able to voice any concerns that you have. You might want to know:

1) Will we have enough money to live on?
2) What if the arrangements don't work? Can we change them?
3) How did you decide on who I should live with?
4) If I can't see Mum/Dad every week, can we talk on the phone?
5) When you are divorced, can I still see both sets of grandparents?

Even if you feel awkward asking questions like these, it is better to have answers than not know what is going on. You need to get a fix on the direction your new life is going to take.

MONEY PROBLEMS

Parents who divorce often experience a drop in their standard of living. Obviously, it is more expensive to run two homes than it is to run one.

It has been found that mothers who had jobs before their marriage broke down cope better with divorce than mothers who were financially dependent on the father. Mothers who did not have jobs may now have to cope not only with adjusting to a new life after the separation and divorce, but with finding a job outside the home too. If you have young brothers or sisters, this can be even harder for your mum as there is very little provision (such as cheap day care facilities) for working mothers in this country.

It is often difficult for parents to separate problems with money from their feelings of anger or distress over the breakup of their relationship. If a father, for example, is not providing the financial support that has been agreed (either informally or by the court), it is hard for the mother (and the child) not to feel that he can't care about them very much if he is creating such hardship. Sometimes mothers in this situation can be tempted to deny the father access.

Fights over child maintenance or their own maintenance can add to a parent's depression and bitterness after separation and divorce. The government's Child Support Agency which assesses child maintenance payments and then enforces payment from the parent who is no longer living with the children, has not inspired confidence since it was set up in 1993 by the inflexible way it has been enforcing maintenance payments. It is hard for parents caught up in these difficulties not to involve their children in problems.

If you are in this situation, it can put you under great strain. You don't want to appear disloyal to the parent who is being forced to take on the whole financial burden and yet you don't want to lose contact with the other parent. Try to let your parents know how you feel about what is going on. The bottom line is that however responsible or irresponsible each of your parents is about money, you still need to spend time with both of them.

Of course, you may have to accept (with good grace if you can), that some of the things you used to take for granted (holidays abroad, a family car and so forth) are no longer possible.

What will life be like after the divorce as you and your parents adjust to the new situation? The next chapter discusses some of the problems you may encounter.

Chapter Six

AFTER THE DIVORCE

It's possible that daily life after your parents' divorce will not be too different from what it was before. Perhaps your parents have been able to sort things out in a friendly way. But even when parents are able to stay on good terms (or perhaps resume being on good terms) there may be problems that surface from time to time.

You may be unfortunate and have parents who remain bitter and angry about what has happened, unable to put the separation and divorce behind them and move forward to make a new life. It is hard to stand back from this and keep remembering that you can't do anything about this and it is nothing to do with you – it just isn't your problem.

Here are some of the difficulties that tend to crop up at this stage of events:

1) *"Each of my parents quizzes me after I've seen the other. I feel as though I'm being turned into a spy. If I tell them anything, they blow it up out of all proportion."*

Your parents are still in the process of "letting go" their former partner and they are therefore bound to be overly interested in her/his new life even if they can't admit it openly. As you are the link between them, it's hard for them to resist pumping you for information. Of course the questions could be just friendly interest, but if you think there are ulterior motives, you're probably right.

When your parents' questions are inappropriate or loaded or the information you give them is then used by them to sound off in a bitter way about what has happened, for example:

"Does this new boyfriend stay the night?"
"How come Mum can afford another holiday?"
"Dad's learning to tap dance! This is the guy who's always hated dancing! I never heard of anything so ridiculous."

then you must tell your parents that they make you feel very uncomfortable. If they want information, they can ask their former partner directly. It's better to put your parents straight in this way than allow yourself to feel trapped, disloyal and full of resentment.

2) *"Since they divorced, Mum and Dad are each trying to buy my affection."*

After a divorce some parents almost seem to compete with each other to buy their child things; it can feel as though they are each trying to get you to like them best.

It could be that they are both trying to make it up to you for the upset and pain of the divorce and they both want to let you know that they love you and that they hope things will be better for you from now on.

If you feel uncomfortable about all this extravagance, you could say to them: "This is nice, but why am I being given so many things?" This might help them to see that you don't need this kind of reassurance while not making you sound ungrateful.

Often it is the parent you don't live with who misses you so much and/or feels guilty that s/he tries to make up for it with endless presents. Of course this often goes down like a lead balloon with the parent you live with who may not be able to afford such treats.

3) *"Mum and Dad won't stop criticising each other to me. I'm sick of listening to them badmouthing each other."*

It's important for you that you can see each of your parents separately without the other parent taking the opportunity to express their bitterness and anger towards that person.

You should not be made to feel by either parent that you have to collude with their view that visiting the other is some kind of dreaded duty that is being forced on you. Neither should you be made to feel that if you enjoy your visit to one parent, you have to keep this part of your life in a separate, secret compartment so that you do not upset the other parent.

Each parent also has to reconcile her/himself to the fact that when you visit their former partner, her/his new boyfriend/girlfriend may also be there.

Right after a divorce, there can be a lot of anger in your parents which keeps bubbling up. It can make you feel like a piggy in the middle – protective towards the parent who is angry and upset and protective towards the parent who is under attack. You may feel obliged to side with the angry parent while secretly sympathising with the attacked parent. This is a wearisome business. Try to maintain a neutral position if you can.

You may worry that one of your parents has become seriously stressed if s/he cannot stop badmouthing their ex-partner and running obsessively over past history again and again. In this case you might suggest to the parent that they need some professional help. Certainly this kind of behaviour is very painful to witness and too difficult for you to try and sort out.

4) *"I used to get on all right with Mum but now that Dad's gone she does nothing but worry and nag. She doesn't seem to realise that I'm growing up. Dad treats me like a grown-up. I wish I could live with him instead."*

In many ways it can be easier to have a good relationship with the parent you don't live with because they don't have to deal with all the day-to-day problems, irritations and demands that the custodial parent has to deal with. If you live with your mum, she has to ensure that you get to bed at a reasonable time, that you do your homework, that you're not snorting cocaine and that there is enough money for the new trainers you need. If seeing dad involves being treated to meals in nice restaurants and bought presents, no wonder you prefer it. But if you lived full-time with your dad, would it really be any different to life with your mother?

Chapter Seven

NEW FAMILY PATTERNS

THE SINGLE-PARENT FAMILY

Following your parents' divorce you may find yourself living with just your mum or just your dad as a single-parent family. Your other parent may be, to all intents and purposes, out of the picture, or just an occasional presence. On the other hand, you may spend weekends or holidays with her/him.

Your mum/dad will probably find it quite hard to adjust to being a single parent. Single parents have to take on the roles of both parents as best they can and when there are problems they have to say no twice. Single parents have no one to discuss immediate problems with. It can be even harder for them if you try to play your other parent off against them ("...but Dad always lets me!"; "Mum wouldn't have minded." etc.)

In a two-parent family that is working well, if you're not getting on with one parent, then the other can often intervene and help sort things out. There can be a good balance. The single parent though, can feel as if s/he is constantly in the firing line with no reinforcements to step in and help.

Single parents are sometimes virtually on their own with their children and they have to cope with loneliness. Of course they need adult friends in the same way you need friends of your own age but it can be hard for them to build new relationships when they also have the responsibility of being a parent. How can they have a social life and be at home for the children?

If you and your mum or dad are a new single-parent family, you can do a lot to help straighten things out when s/he is struggling. By this, I don't mean that you should start trying to protect the parent you live with or run her/his life. S/he needs space just like you do.

A single parent also has to spread her/himself round all the children if you have sisters and brothers. You may find it harder to get time and attention for yourself.

What might be helpful when you are adjusting to being a single-parent family is to have fortnightly "meetings" at which you discuss how things are going and what problems have arisen. This can be a very practical discussion and it can also clear the air if tension has been building up.

There are probably simple things you can do to help such as offering to baby-sit for your younger brothers/sisters every Friday or make the dinner on Tuesdays. Things like this will give your mum/dad a break.

It's also a good idea if you and your mum/dad do something together on a regular basis which you both enjoy. It could be going swimming or even just watching a favourite TV programme together. Things like this can strengthen your relationship as people rather than as parent/child and it's also good to know that you each think the other is fun to be with.

KEEPING IN TOUCH WITH THE NON-CUSTODIAL PARENT

"Dad said he'd always be there when I needed him. But when I have nightmares, I can't call him up in the middle of the night and say 'I'm having a nightmare'. It's just no good."
Damian (10)

"Other children have their dad every day. It's just not fair."
Judith (8)

The parent you don't live with will be finding it hard to adjust to not seeing you every day. It's also very hard for you.

This parent will soon realise that in practice, s/he now has very little say over your life on a day-to-day basis. This can make her/him feel very out of touch and anxious. Hopefully, you are able to be in touch with her/him on a regular basis. Perhaps you spend the weekends with her/him or school holidays or you meet up every so often. Again, it's good to try and spend some time doing something together which you both enjoy.

You may find that the amount of time you have with this non-custodial parent just doesn't feel enough. It's difficult to cram into a weekend or a few hours all the news and

affection and love that would have been spread over a week. You may find yourself feeling tearful and upset when it is time to say good-bye. If this is the case, you might ask if it's possible to spend more time with her/him as you don't feel you are getting enough.

Of course, it can also be tricky to have two homes. If you want, say, to see school friends at the weekend but you have to go and stay with your father in another town, you can end up feeling both resentful and guilty.

In this situation it helps enormously if your parents are able to communicate amicably and to be generous and flexible in the way they arrange access. You also need to speak up for yourself and say what you would like to happen. Arrangements that may have worked very well when you were ten may no longer be appropriate when you are thirteen.

YOUR PARENTS' NEW RELATIONSHIPS

Now that your mum and dad have separated they are free to enter into new relationships. Of course, they may have already done so and perhaps this was why the marriage broke up.

But even if this was the case, your mum and dad are now free from the conflicts that existed in their marriage to establish new relationships on a different footing. One of these may eventually lead to another marriage or long-term partnership.

Some parents feel very battered by the breakup of their marriage and try to make themselves feel better by starting new relationships before they are really ready for them. This is something that will sort itself out in time.

You will probably have very mixed feelings about your mum or dad having a new relationship. Part of you may feel relieved that they are starting to enjoy themselves again and carve out a new life. But part of you may worry that if they find a new partner, you may become unloved and unwanted. This is because children tend to interpret the divorce of their parents as in some way a rejection of them, instead of what it really is – the rejection of a husband by a wife or a wife by a husband. It is not the rejection of a child by its parents.

You may have had to play a very supportive role with your mum or dad in the weeks following the separation and divorce and have become very close to her/him. Perhaps you worry that if s/he has a new adult relationship it will destroy this closeness.

If you take a strong dislike to a parent's new girlfriend or boyfriend, it is worth asking yourself whether you really dislike her/him (which is quite possible), or whether your feelings stem from anxieties such as these about your relationship with your mum or dad and how secure you feel. It's also easy to compare this person with your mum/dad, and find them wanting.

A new relationship may also be upsetting for you because it means that your mum and dad will not be reunited one day. However unlikely this possibility was, some part of you may have been hoping that it would happen.

It is hard for the parent you live with to establish a new relationship at her/his own pace. Because of family responsibilities, s/he may have to introduce a new boyfriend/ girlfriend to you before s/he would have ideally wished to. S/he will probably be aware that you look with some anxiety at each new person s/he brings home, wondering if this is a potential stepfather or stepmother.

The parent you don't live with has an easier time in this respect as s/he is freer to date and build relationships in private.

If you want to check out how serious your mum or dad's current relationship is, why not ask? You should of course be understanding if s/he is gradually finding out for her/himself and not in a position to give a definite answer.

STEPPARENTS AND REMARRIAGE

"Despite all the aggro you hear about stepfathers, mine meant a good deal to me. Once I heard my mother laughing, my stepfather would have had to work very hard to do wrong by me. I wanted him because she wanted him."

Child care expert Penelope Leach, April 1994

"I remember hating Tony, my stepfather, with every fibre of my being. And I hated Mum too, for agreeing to marry him. When she and Dad divorced, she told me it was just the two of us.

*When she told me she was marrying Tony, it
was instant hate."*
Annabelle (14)

A stepfamily is formed when two partners
come together, one or both of whom bring
children, either full-time or part-time, from a
previous relationship.

Stepfamilies used to get a very bad press.
Think of Cinderella's unkind stepmother and
stepsisters and Snow White's wicked
stepmother. These stepfamilies came into being
following the death of the first wife, often in
childbirth. The prefix "step" comes from the old
English word "stoep" which means
bereavement. Snow White's mother, you will
remember, died in childbirth while Cinderella
was in still in mourning for her dead mother.
Today, the majority of stepfamilies come into
being when parents divorce or separate from
their first partners.

There are about two million children and
young people growing up in a stepfamily in
Britain. In the USA there are 15 million. Most
of these children live with their mother and her
new partner, their stepfather. Many visit their
father who may also have a new partner, their
stepmother, at the weekends and holidays. But
there are a great many possible combinations
of stepfamilies.

ACCOMMODATING YOU

Adjusting to the idea of your mum or dad remarrying or setting up a new long-term relationship can be difficult.

First of all, it's important to keep in mind that this new stepfamily is not supposed to blot out your old family. The memories and relationships you have from that first family cannot be taken away from you.

If one of your parents is dead, you can still continue to think about and talk about her/him.

If you currently visit or stay with the parent you don't live with, or talk to him/her on the phone, there is no reason why this should not continue. Your new stepmum or stepdad is not supposed to replace your real parent.

A stepfamily cannot be a tight, closed unit – by definition it involves children who have loyalties and ties in two different places and it must therefore have a fluid structure that can accommodate these links.

FINDING OUT ABOUT THE MARRIAGE

When your parent is considering marriage or setting up a long-term relationship, it is good if this can be discussed with you beforehand, not just sprung on you. This remarriage is an important landmark for you too and you need to have an opportunity to talk through what it means.

Of course, it may not happen in a clear cut way, Sometimes new relationships just evolve with your mum/dad and their new boyfriend/girlfriend gradually spending more and more time together until it seems more sensible to live together. This can be a good way to do it from your point of view as it gives you an opportunity to get to know this new person.

WORRIES AND FEARS

Your mum/dad is probably very happy and excited about her/his plans for life with a new partner but you may not feel the same way. You may have all kinds of worries:

"Will I still be wanted and needed in this new set-up?"
As a small child you were used to a particular family pattern that lasted until your parents separated. You may then have had to adjust to a single-parent family pattern.

A child who lives with a single parent often finds her/himself being treated by that parent as an ally in a hostile world. You become the one whose job it is to stick up for and look after your mum/dad. You behave more like a friend to that parent than their child.

Now that mum/dad has a new partner, you may feel that your role as protector has been usurped and you have been made redundant. It's certainly very unfair if a parent relies on a child to look after her/him after their divorce but then disregards the child's feelings when a new partner appears on the scene.

If you were very close to your mum/dad, you may find that there will be quite a transition period as you and your parent become close in a different way that puts less burden on you.

This can only be good for you – at your age it is more appropriate for you to be putting your energies into developing your relationships with your friends. It may be quite a relief to know that you no longer need to support and worry about your mum/dad.

"You're not my dad / mum!"
It's tempting to say this to a stepparent if you feel they are overdoing their parental role. It can be particularly difficult if this stepparent was the reason your mum and dad split up in the first place.

Of course a stepparent is not your natural parent and can't replace or be exactly like that natural parent. Acknowledging this could make it easier for your stepmum/dad to behave in a warm, concerned but more detached way towards you – more like an adult friend.

On the other hand, the two adults in a stepfamily, your parent and her/his partner, have to be able to work together as a parental team enforcing the same rules and standards. It's tempting to try and prise them apart by playing divide and rule but you will actually feel more secure if they do present a united front. (See the discussion on family rules below.)

"What shall I call her/him?"
You already have a mum and dad. Why not call
your stepmum/stepdad by their first name.

"What if I don't love my stepdad/stepmum?"
Why should you love him/her? You both need
time to get to know each other. It's sensible to
start with the idea that you may not love your
parent's new partner. Then it can come as a
pleasant surprise if you do find you like
him/her.

*"Will my stepdad/stepmum be allowed to tell
me what to do?"*
Remember that it's not easy for your parent
and his/her new partner to bring together two
families or one family and an outsider at the
same time as they are developing their own
relationship. The normal sequence of events
that lead to family life – courtship, marriage,
children – is out of sync a second time around
with children already there from the beginning.

This means that lots of important things,
like family rules, tend to be thought about on
the hoof instead of being agreed ahead of time.
Here are some potential flashpoints that will
need thinking about:

1. FAMILY RULES AND SANCTIONS
Your parent and stepparent need to be in
agreement about what these rules are, and

what sanctions are to be applied if they are broken (no TV; no staying out; etc.). It's also important that rules and sanctions are applied consistently so that you don't feel that your stepbrothers/stepsisters are more favoured or vice versa.

2. RESPECT
Your parent and stepparent should respect your feelings of loyalty to your other parent. However fed up they feel about what s/he has or has not done, they should not go on about it in front of you.

You should respect your parent's choice of new partner. You might not like her/him but your parent obviously does. Try to give her/him a break and don't pick on everything s/he does and says all the time.

3. CHORES AND SCHEDULES
It's helpful to everyone in a new stepfamily if exactly what chores everyone is expected to do is worked out so there are no misunderstandings. It's also good if things like bedtimes, TV watching, homework time, time in the bathroom, etc. are sorted out.

4. COMPETITIVE FEELINGS
Maybe your stepmum isn't as good at cooking as your mum; maybe your stepdad doesn't know as much about animals as your dad;

maybe your stepbrother is better at music than you are; maybe you're better at swimming than he is. In a new stepfamily, where there is a maze of relationships to sort out, you would be a saint if you didn't sometimes feel some hostile competitiveness towards your stepparent, stepbrothers and stepsisters and some malicious pleasure when they don't do things as well as you're used to.

What is needed is tolerance and a good sense of humour as the family begins to blend together and allows everyone to be themselves.

5. SPACE

New stepmothers or stepfathers often come complete with stepsisters and/or stepbrothers too. If space is tight you may find yourself having to share a bedroom. Try to do it with good grace. There are imaginative ways that you can keep your own space – perhaps a partition or curtain.

Perhaps your stepsisters/stepbrothers don't live with you all the time but spend weekends and holidays or perhaps you're the one who has to go and stay in a household where your stepbrothers and stepsisters live permanently. In this situation it's hard not to feel either invaded or that you are somehow intruding.

A good solution, if there isn't enough space for each person to have her/his own room, is for

each child to at least have a drawer or cupboard or shelf of their own. That way everyone can be sure of finding their things safely where they left them next time they stay.

HOW WILL YOU GET ON WITH YOUR STEPBROTHERS/ STEPSISTERS?

There is an expectation, or rather a hope, that children in a new stepfamily will become instant friends.

Obviously this is difficult enough even with brothers and sisters that you have grown up with. Give yourselves time to get to know each other and try to be tolerant. A stepfamily can be a hotbed of jealousy, rivalry and resentment or a melting pot of very different people who can appreciate and enjoy each other's particularities.

There are other complications that need adjusting to. If you are the oldest child, you may suddenly find that you aren't any more. A boy with two sisters may now also have three brothers. An only child may find her/himself suddenly part of a large family.

A complication that may not have occurred to you is that you may get along with a stepsister/stepbrother of your own age a little too well. However attractive you find each other, it's just not a good idea to start any kind of girlfriend/boyfriend relationship within a stepfamily. The complications and long-term problems are just too great. Don't allow yourself to be tempted.

AND A NEW BABY?

The arrival of a new half-sister or half-brother in a stepfamily can be a great pleasure for everyone. The new baby can also make everyone feel closer since s/he provides a blood link. If the baby is adopted s/he also provides a link by virtue of being a new addition to the family. The baby's arrival reaffirms the strong bond between your parent and stepparent.

On the other hand, if you feel insecure or unhappy in your stepfamily, the arrival of a half-brother or half-sister may make you feel even more excluded. You may worry that your parent and stepparent have their "own" family and you are not a real part of it.

Of course every child, whether s/he is in a natural family or in a stepfamily, fears being displaced by a new baby. To some extent these fears are justified – new babies are very demanding and take up a lot of time and parental energy. Try to distinguish between fears like these which all older siblings feel about a new arrival and see if your feelings of insecurity in fact have nothing to do with the baby. Why not talk to your parent about them if you can or to some other sympathetic adult?

A NEW FAMILY STYLE

A new stepfamily is a challenge but one that has lots of potential for good things to happen – if you and everyone else will let them. It can provide emotional stability if the two adults at its centre are confident and directive. It can also provide a diversity of enriching relationships.

A stepfamily needs to blend and evolve its own style. You may find that it will be the little things that count.

Whether you open Christmas presents at breakfast time on Christmas day or after dinner, for example, is the kind of thing that needs to be discussed as does whether someone with a birthday gets to have breakfast in bed.

Rituals like these that you enjoy can cause a lot of upset if they are not done in the way you so take for granted you didn't realise you did. It's a good idea to try and anticipate them and perhaps discuss starting new family traditions or mixing some of those from each family that has come together.

STRETCHING YOUR WINGS

"There never used to be puddings."
  Mark (9)

"Mum never used to go sailing."
  Rose (15)

"Dad always said he hated trainers and now he's wearing them."
  Ramesh (12)

You may find that your mum or dad, who never used to show any interest in, say, gardening, suddenly takes it up with enthusiasm because her/his new partner is a keen gardener.

You can choose to see this as your parent becoming hopelessly dominated by their new partner or you could see it as your parent seizing the opportunity to stretch her/his wings and try out all the new experiences and pleasures now available.

There may be good things that your new stepfamily can provide that weren't available to you before – allow yourself to enjoy them.

"They're not my real family. Why should I care about them?"
Winston (13)

It is a sad fact that in our society where divorce is so commonplace, children are still being brought up to believe that loving and caring is only appropriate in relation to members of their "natural" family. This can lead to a sad and confusing state of affairs for you if your parents then divorce and you are later expected to settle down in a new family structure with a stepparent and perhaps stepsiblings. Is it OK to like, care about, perhaps love these people or not?

Of course it may be that however hard you try, you just don't care for your stepmum or you can't bear your stepbrother. No one is saying that you have to like them although it's nice if you do.

The important thing is that you allow yourself to be open to the possibility of liking your stepfamily and of their liking you. Of course this does not mean that you are being disloyal to the parent you don't live with. People can love different people in different ways. You can love, say, your stepmum without taking anything away from the deep love you feel for your natural mum.

TAKING CONTROL

Even in the best-handled separations or divorces, children usually feel hurt, frightened, anxious and upset. The life you are used to has disappeared and perhaps you do not yet know whether your new life is going to provide you with all the security and support and care that you need.

Acknowledging your fears, discussing them and thinking about them can help you take more control over your life at this difficult time when events are so much out of your control. Be kind to yourself and give yourself time to adjust and time to heal.

Chapter Eight

QUESTIONS AND ANSWERS

Q. After my dad moved out, my little brother started wetting the bed again. I find it hard to pay attention at school and last week I got into a fight with someone, about nothing really. I don't think things will ever feel right again.

A. The tension, anxiety and upset children feel when their parents separate show themselves in different ways depending how old you are.

Small children, like your brother, will often start behaving in a more babyish way, perhaps clinging a lot and wetting the bed again.

Older children sometimes find their anger and upset bubbles up when they don't expect it and they get into fights at school or behave aggressively. Concentrating on school work can be difficult because all your emotional energy is being directed at the problem of your mum and dad splitting up and how you feel about it.

This difficult stage won't last for ever. In the meantime, comfort your little brother by being affectionate and by carrying on doing routine things with him. Comfort yourself by talking to your brothers/sisters of your own age if you have them, to a good friend or to a trusted adult who will understand how you feel.

Q. *My mum and dad split up because my mum used to have rages and smash things and yell at my dad. Now that I live with just my dad it's peaceful but I want to see my mum. Is that wrong?*

A. It is not wrong to miss your mum. Even when parents have lots of faults, there are still good things about them that you miss. If you are not in any way at risk from your mum's behaviour, it may be that you can continue to have a relationship with her. Hopefully, your dad will understand that even if he doesn't want to see her anymore, it's natural that you do. Why not talk to him about it?

Q. *My stepfather is always shouting at me and finding fault with what I do or say. When I'm wearing my nightie or pyjamas, I don't like the way he looks at me. It makes me feel uncomfortable. What should I do?*

A. Sexual tensions can arise in a stepfamily from all sides – parent/stepchild or stepbrother/stepsister. Tensions rarely turn into actual sexual abuse (although of course sexual abuse can occur in a stepfamily as it can in a natural family).

It's possible that your stepfather is cross with you so often because he too feels uncomfortable and he wants to keep his distance. Why not tell your mum that you don't like your stepdad seeing you in your nightie and you want more privacy. This will alert her to the sexual tension in the air and she will be able to diffuse it safely.

However, if you feel at risk of abuse or you have been abused by a stepparent or by your mum's boyfriend you should tell your mum or another adult you trust what has happened and get help. If you have no one to talk to, call one of the helplines listed at the back of this book.

Q. *My dad comes to the house to collect me for the weekends. He and Mum start talking in the kitchen in a snappy, tense way and they always get into an argument about money. It makes me feel sick with anxiety. I don't enjoy the weekend after that.*

A. Let your parents know how upsetting you find this. They should try to behave better. Rows about money should be had when you're not around.

Q. My stepmum always lets her children get away with things but with me and my sister she is very strict. When I said it wasn't fair she said she treated us all the same. This isn't true.

A. It's very possible that your stepmum thinks she treats you all the same but she in fact favours her own children. It's hard for any adult to treat other children equally with their own because they are so tuned in to their own children. But of course, it would be very unfair if your stepmum didn't try to behave equally towards you all. Of course your dad must also try to include his stepchildren equally alongside you and your sister in the same way. It's good that you stuck up for yourself and complained.

Q. When my gran comes to stay she brings me a present but not one for my stepbrother. He gets cross with me about it but it's not my fault.

A. No, it's not your fault and it's a pity your grandmother is so unimaginative about your stepbrother's feelings. Of course she may not be aware of the bad situation she is creating. Perhaps you could ask your parent to explain to her how uncomfortable this situation is making you feel – or perhaps you feel you can raise it with your gran yourself. If you don't get

103

anywhere, you could make it clear that in future any present she brings will be shared between you and your stepbrother.

Q. *My parents separated because my mum decided she is gay. I don't understand how a married woman with a child can become gay.*

A. If a mum or dad tells their child that s/he is gay (a lesbian or a homosexual), this can be a big shock. On the other hand, you may have known for some time that your dad or mum is gay. (A gay person is someone who is sexually attracted to people of their own sex rather than to people of the opposite sex. It is thought that about one person in ten is gay.)

People don't decide to be gay or decide to be straight (heterosexual). A person's sexual orientation may be something they are born with or it may result from early childhood socialisation or it may be a combination of these things. No one yet knows quite how this works.

Society still has a very uninformed and prejudiced attitude to homosexuality (although things are better than they used to be). This means that information about homosexuality is not easily available to support people who think they may be gay. They may try to deny this part of themselves or simply not be in a position to identify what it is. It is also the case that some people are just not aware of their "true" sexual orientation until they are well into adult life – and sometimes married and/or a parent.

This does not mean that your gay parent now wishes that you hadn't come along. In fact, many people who have known that they are gay from adolescence, long to be or contrive to become parents. Your mum or dad is not less of a parent because s/he is gay.

For a parent to discover that s/he is gay can sometimes be a tremendous crisis, particularly if it results in the breakup of a marriage. S/he would not have chosen the difficult situation they find themselves in. Your parent will be glad to know that you still love her/him.

Discovering that your parent is homosexual can be difficult because it is less easy to find sympathetic and well-informed people with whom to share this information. Don't expose yourself to hurt by telling ignorant or prejudiced people what has happened. A counsellor or helpline can offer help and support if you don't have the right person available to talk to.

Chapter Nine

WHERE TO GET HELP AND ADVICE

When you feel upset or need help, try to talk to someone you trust – perhaps your parents, your friends, your grandparents or your teacher. If you don't have anyone to talk to, you could ring a helpline. A sympathetic adult will take your call and you can talk in complete confidence

HELPLINES
These help and advice phone lines are free (you don't need a phone card or money, just dial the number) and open 24 hours:

CHILDLINE 0800 1111

THE SAMARITANS 0345 909090

ORGANISATIONS THAT YOUR PARENTS MIGHT FIND HELPFUL

CHILD POVERTY ACTION GROUP
Advice and help for low-income families.
1 Bath Street
London EC1V 9DX
tel: 071 253 3406

CHILDREN'S LEGAL CENTRE
20 Compton Terrace
London N1 2UN
tel: 071 359 6251

THE CHILDREN'S SOCIETY
(formerly the Church of England Children's Society)
The Society offers support to children and families under pressure.
Edward Rudolf House
Margery Street
London WC1X OJL
tel: 071 837 4299

DIVORCE CONCILIATION AND ADVISORY SERVICE
38 Ebury Street
London SW1W OLU
tel: 071 730 2422

GINGERBREAD

A national self-help association for one-parent families. It has a network of local groups and advice leaflets for parents on a number of problems:
35 Wellington Street
London WC2E 7BN
tel: 071 240 0953

NATIONAL COUNCIL FOR ONE PARENT FAMILIES

A national charity which advises individuals and government on all matters to do with single parent families (eg family law; employment; tax; poverty etc).
255 Kentish Town Road
London NW5 2LX
tel: 071 267 1361

NATIONAL STEPFAMILY ASSOCIATION

72 Willesden Lane
London NW6 7TA
tel: 071 372 0844

RELATE (formerly the Marriage Guidance Council)

This organisation helps adults with marital problems and it also helps couples to separate if the relationship cannot be saved. The national headquarters will advise on the nearest office to you:

Herbert Gray College
Little Church Street
Coventry CV21 3AP
tel: Rugby 573241

SCOTTISH COUNCIL FOR SINGLE
PARENTS
The Council offers advice, information and
referral.
44 Albany Street
Edinburgh EH1 3QR
tel: 031 556 3899

TAVISTOCK CLINIC
An NHS out-patient clinic which promotes the
mental health of families.
120 Belsize Lane
London NW3 5BA
tel: 071 435 7111

BOOKS FOR CHILDREN
Some of these titles are out of print but may
still be available in libraries.

UNDER FIVES

I Have Two Homes
(divorced parents)
Althea Braithwaite
(Dinosaur)

The Visitors Who Came to Stay
(about a stepfamily)
Annalena McAlfee and Anthony Browne
(Hamish Hamilton)

Jafta – My Father
(not strictly about divorce but about longing for
an absent father)
Hugh Lewin and Lisa Kopper
(Hamish Hamilton)

Children Don't Divorce
Rosemary Stones and Nicola Spoor
(Dinosaur)

6 – 8 YEAR OLDS

Dinosaurs Divorce
Laurie Krasny Brown and Marc Brown
(Collins)

What Am I Doing in a Stepfamily?
Claire Berman and Dick Wilson
(Angus & Robertson)

8 – 10 YEAR OLDS

Ugly Mug
(about a child and his divorced parents)
Annie Dalton
(Hamish Hamilton Antelopes)

It's Not the End of the World
(coming to terms with divorce)
Judy Blume
(Pan)

Instant Sisters
(stepsisters who even have to share a room)
Rose Impey
(Lions)

12 YEARS AND UPWARDS

Fat Chance
Twelve-year-old overweight Tessa hopes that
dad will come back if she manages to lose
weight...
Jacqueline Roy
(Blackie)

My Family and Other Natural Disasters
A thirteen-year-old's view of his
parents'separation. Lively, funny and
sympathetic.
Josephine Feeney
(Viking)

Goggle Eyes
(a stepfather finds he can nothing right...)
Anne Fine
(Hamish Hamilton)

Step by Wicked Step
(children from an amazing variety of families
compare notes)
Anne Fine
(Hamish Hamilton)

Madame Doubtfire
A father will do anything to be with his
children...
Anne Fine
(Hamish Hamilton)

BOOKS FOR PARENTS

The Which Guide to Divorce
Helen Garlick
(Which Books)

Helping Children Cope with Divorce
Rosemary Wells
(Sheldon Press)

A Step-Parent's Handbook
Kate Raphael
(Sheldon Press)

Divorce and Your Children
Anne Hooper
(Robson Books)

INDEX